Fallen Prose

Steven Schroeder

VIRTUAL ARTISTS COLLECTIVE
http://www.vacteam.com
ISBN 0-9772974-1-1

"Signs," "Deltas of Forgetfulness," "Far Enough," "Time and Again," "High Places," "Bright," "Fluency," "Where to Strike," "Like This," "Born Old," "Guangdonghua, Macao," "Starting Here," and "The Tree in Guimiao Village," were first published in *Writing Macao*. "Cities of Conversation," "Elegance," "Parable," and "They Fly," were first published in *Moon City Review*.

Cover design by Steven Schroeder, from a photo taken in Shenzhen

Fallen Prose

Table of Contents

Parable

In the South, sticky sweet summer heat
entices everything that grows to an orgy.
Lichi leave orchards in June, gather in flesh pots,
alligator red skin on skin, soft sweet
nectar on tiptoe just beneath the surface,
all anticipation for the moment it will break free
and touch the world; and there are wicker baskets
full at the bottom of stairways, bags and boxes
in every office. They drop, plop, at your feet,
manna from a shockingly promiscuous
heaven dispersed by armies a thousand times
ten thousand strong on foot enlisted to scatter
seeds without knowing they are carriers.
Fruit tempts with no assistance from
subtle serpent theologians, and no one believes
they can be booted from this garden, which promises
to go on and on and on forever, world without end.
      A worker preparing for a day of hard labor
puts his pick down, strips off his shirt, strips
skin from half a dozen one by one, kisses down
pulp, spits seeds into a flower bed where

---

they will grow. Some seed falls on rock, some
on paving stone. Some sprouts and grows, comes
again, entices other orgies other times.

      And careless walkers and walkers
who have despaired of finding a moment lichi-free
for feet, grind the sweet pulp into the faint odor
of sugary decay that permeates Southern places
in summer, a molasses-coated world you can
sink into with no sign
of ice, no expectation
of winter.

Lichi

Undress soft sweet flesh
in summer heat gently
with your fingertips.
                    Eat. This
body on your tongue
dissolves
thirst.

Human

For three days, this

signal has been

frozen on

walk don't

walk green

red.

      Walkers do

what it says: go

don't go. It is

      an icon, a

deity suspended,

human, waiting.

Zion

High places
are brought low, not
because some old god
is jealous of what
is worshiped there, but
because they can be sold.
      Mountains are
the leading export
here. Highway unrolls
to make way for impatient
trucks that move rock to fill
ocean.
      No need to climb
Zion. It comes down
one stone at a time.

A Wormhole in Zhuhai

Passing from China
           to China to China
requires something like
a wormhole in Zhuhai,
and the gravitational distortion
of that singularity bends light
all the way to Shekou.
Mouth to mouth, Guanyin
to Kun Iam, two colonies
under compassionate eyes
that do not overlook semi
colonialism, one history,
four languages, ten
thousand interpretations.

They Fly

There are sleepers along the walk,
stripped to the waist in heat
that does not break
even when it rains. It rolled in
at the beginning of May and has
crushed the last parasol of resistance
by the end of June.
               Some of them
worked through the night on this
city that has no idea how to stop. Some
will rise soon to begin again,
tearing the city down by hand with pick
and hammer, while massive
trucks wait in line to pour concrete
where the Phoenix city rises
as it falls, a Daoist geometry
of solid contraries. Some
will gather at the edges of rich people's haunts
and scratch for leavings as they pass.

There are little armies marching on
these same edges with sticks
they carry to keep the rabble in
line, ensure that money is never disturbed.
There are moments of contact; where a cop
and a beggar have waited on the same corner
for years, there is a strategic admiration
like that between commanders who face each other
on the same battlefield a long time, intimate
as lovers. The longer the war, the more
it resembles a lover's quarrel.
                    I have seen cops and beggars
trade smiles and conversation after
coins have dropped and another tourist has
gone away undisturbed. They have roles
to play, and the drama, like the city, does
not sleep for fear it will not wake. When
a coin drops in a beggar's bowl, it is
the sound of money, rhythmic as picks
and hammers at scenes of endless construction:
tear the city down, raise the city up, let us
make a city. There are sleepers, but never the city.

Three young teens have brought a skateboard
to practice on the wide open square at *hai shang shie jie* –
almost too early to vogue, but a cop not much older
than they watches with a look that says he would
join them if he could. He will send them away
when the square is crowded with tourists
and young mothers who bring their children
here to walk. But not now. A man who must be forty-
something stops, hand on hip *contrapposto*, to watch them.
              He can remember a moment like this
if he holds himself still against the money. But still
is possible only for an instant at the pivot point
on which the world turns. He moves, and so
do the boys with the skateboard.

A mother laughs with her daughter
in a bright orange dress, shows her how
to flap her wings, and, trailing tiny
bells of laughter,
they fly.

Medicine

Sound breathed
day in day out becomes
the texture of the page
where sound is written,
and you can hear
the poison haze
that gathers on
the damp air
of this southern coast.
Horn blast as truck passes
on Nanhailu tastes bitter
after sweet sunrise song
of bulbuls, and sour
red hibiscus flower
mutters at the babble
of sandals in its ear,
so many yesterday
they broke the split bamboo
rail that edges the walk
and rendered the line between
path and border porous. Here

and there, a flower crushed
under stray steps leaves a stain
of salty blood, and the whole mess
tastes like medicine an old woman
who has read your tongue
mixed to cure you.

Counting

Walking against a shift change,
the human dimension of number dawns
slowly.
          Every body north against my south,
it is no use counting.
One by one obscures the one
of many. One of many is
a human face that does not turn
at the turning of the turning
world. Count: one. One,
turning the world in its image.

A young woman stands on the edge
of the walk, watching.
She wears an orange tee
that says *I Love NY*. I don't know
if she loves what she sees, but she
expects something, someone, of it,
a face turning to her turning. Another
woman walks south to the gate of a factory
with an empty bucket swinging on one hip.

She does not
have the air of a woman rushing to fill it,
sways Sisyphean with this passing moment
of emptiness. A man in a yellow hard hat
crouches by the walk gazing at a building
that has been rising for weeks on his back,
takes a long drag before he stands.
         Yellow leaves on gray
paving stone where the crowd breaks, passes,
not one and one and one, but
one. No use counting.

Like This

Even over the sound of traffic,
the sound of gathering
desire,
you can hear every revolution
of some bicycle wheels
as they make their way
among walkers on this busy street.
Even the well-oiled scream
at sudden stops. Most are
so heavy they
lurch on crooked paths
while riders attend entirely to
not falling. If socialism
comes, they said
before the fall in Chile,
it comes on bicycle. When
it comes, it comes
like this.

Where to Strike

An iron hook drops slowly
from a height that will be
ten stories when the building
rises there, dangling from a crane
that pivots steps from a busy
sidewalk in remembrance
of the fishermen who worked
this place before it became
land. No one looks up, thinks
about the crushing weight
over their heads. A weary woman
and a weary man become
part of the landscape between
sidewalk and street, heads on knees,
eyes emptied, a box between them
that might contain all they own
or all they have to sell. The walk
has been made new in a week
for the benefit of those with larger boxes
who will scarcely walk on it but prefer
red brick herringbone to worn gray

paving stones below their windows.

       Watching the workers

who put down the brick, I attend

to the making of edges – straight curbs

of gray tight against red triangles – and recall

how my grandfather knew in his hands

where to strike the brick and at what angle

to break it in a clean line to fill

space right up to the edge.

Shaken

for Xiaohong

Buddha is an old woman with bound feet.
Almost a hundred years etched in a web
drawn over a face set against a life of pain.
Blind eyes pierce mine looking for a sign
by which to know me.

      I kneel at her feet with a recorder while
she prays a hundred times, once for each bead
on a string held by hands that have bent
too long to survival.

        A crooked finger caresses
a bead with each prayer; prayer passes
to her life. She repeats her life a hundred times,
a hundred times, fingering each memory
strung on living held by hands bent
too long to survival. You open my ears
in a whisper, a whisper, her
life repeating in three tongues. *All suffering*,
she says, *all suffering*.

And when I press what cost me nothing
into her hand, she repeats *thankyou thankyou*
Buddha will bless you. All is suffering,
she says. And suffering is the offspring
of desire. She has waited all her life
for Buddha to appear. Shaken, not
enlightened, we will hold each other
and pass this on.

Drowning

Three iridescent beetles
upended by yesterday's rain
arc across the lines of a broken
paving stone, gray. They are
swimmers drowning in air,
gasping for last breaths
but unable to surface.
                    A yellow leaf,
dry, settles beside them
without a struggle.

Signs

The walk is
a gray stone grid
laid by a thousand hands
broken here and there
by a crack where
earth has settled or
paused to take a breath.
      One that angles
from this side to the other
might be a memory
of a southern tremor
that swept the ocean over
a coast that could have been
this one, concrete meditation
on death that escapes the notice
of most passersby.
      A thin stain of oil
inscribes the wavering
path of a bicycle slowed
out of control some time ago
by a staggering crowd. It takes

earth breathing and memory
to break stone, but a scrap
of paper, a leaf on wind,
a hat, a begging bowl can
break the grid. Sweepers
set to work before the sun
to move them. Signs
of human presence –
rigid patterns broken
at the drop of a hat, armies
to fix them in stone, control
out of control on every edge.

Born Old

This city, fashioned from cinders
of stars that fell when they became too tired
to fly, was born old. She rises early,
sits at the mirror for hours covering every blemish
with layers of forgetfulness before
she steps out on a street crowded
with people too busy to notice, thick
with clouds of obsession that are hard
to swallow and make the air
heavy as water in all weather. She catches
sight of herself in a window on the street, sees
cinders and a sparkle of stardust
where damp memory has worn forgetfulness away.

Coaxing

A woman is mopping
the square at *hai shang shi jie*,
the same one who struggled three
days ago in a downpour
to hold back rising water
with her broom.

      These omnipresent sweepers
are miracles of nature, relentlessly
attending to order veiled under city
chaos, coaxing it to light, coaxing
sun awake to begin another day.

Fluency

On every corner, there is someone selling
a copy watch or a tailored suit
and my Western face is promising,
though I haven't worn a watch in thirty years
and have never owned a tailored suit. But here
the face, not the clothes, make the man,
so I have consumer potential. I am late,
trying to weave through dense crowds
to the ferry. They say people are always
in a hurry in Hong Kong, but
it is a hard place to hurry.
       Back in Shekou, I walk
the short block
where women wait
in doorways
every evening, voices
smooth in English,
finding their mark.

Nothing Seems Close

rises in sparks with steps on paving stones,
rolls off traffic that doubles every day,
settles with clouds that have taken up residence
in low hills around the city. In faces
set on one thing or another, gray between
bright and dark softens everything, melts hard lines
until nothing seems close, smells of diesel,
leaves you breathless longing for mountains.

Starting Here

Two hours into the haze
that settled out of the last
century over the beginning of this
one and found all at once
this morning, a cool breeze
struggles over from the ocean
and tunnels random paths for light.
Heat drips right through, backs up
in streets that have no provision
to drain such floods, mixes
with factory ash to make mud
that mucks up every step
with what remains of the day
before, seeps through skin, turns
bones into solid impossibilities of ice,
laughs at reason's puzzlement, slows
the pace of the world starting here
until its motion cannot be distinguished
from the full stop of a granite mountain.

Morning Raga

Weather has transported soldiers here
to some northern frontier
in long wool coats
and fur-trimmed hats
fighting cold and boredom
while armies in another war
stream past on bicycles
fashioned from iron meant to
withstand broken pavement
and collisions.
       The black-windowed black
Lexus sweeping them aside
in company with endless repetitions
of a horn droning beneath the steady tabla
of the engine's morning raga
must contain some general
ready to order them all to die
with a wave of his hand. Cold has
no place here and will be gone
tomorrow, but boredom will not

withdraw before it has driven

every army of occupation to distraction.

It Will Stay

Sky settled grayheavy over morning
hours before sunrise. Hibiscus
flowers hang exhausted from holding
it til it lightened and rose
encouraged by birds
who were up early looking
for light and feasting
on fat worms washed to the surface
by rain.
        People huddle against chill
illusion while sun shines on the other
side of clouds, makes gray glow, break
at intervals, but fails to convince
it will stay.

Deltas of Forgetfulness

Better eyes would know
the next construction site
by the gathering of outsiders
in moments before it rises.
The city grows in clusters
of foreign bodies. One
floating city on an ocean
planet deposits silt in deltas
of forgetfulness. Eyes,
sites of memory, move with it,
determined to see it whole.

Solitary

In the matter of mountains,
                    it is the idea
that draws crowds. Rapids and rockslides
are problems of human engineering; they
pose material questions, gravitational
challenges; throw themselves in the way
of speeding cities; run amok.

                    Masses wait
while they are smoothed, admire them
on postcards where they lie flat
and rarely induce queasiness.
A spacehungry species
with command of machines
moves them to make way, imagines
stockpiles poised to fill oceans,
manufactures human-scaled replicas
in parks below high-rise cities,
builds museums to contain
improbable images of old poets
solitary on mountains untamed.

Nomads

Southern cities make spaces for nomads
in spite of themselves. Where Nanhai meets Binhai,
the overpass makes a roof, and a man sleeps
flat on his back until some wandering messiah
with a badge orders him to take up his bed
and walk. Another lies fetal by the path
in the shadow of a four star hotel, hard
hat on his head, covered with a plastic bag.
He will rise to work on another skyscraper, dream
of living in it, but hope for unintended corners
where those uprooted can escape the rain and
snatch a moment undisturbed – the same thing
wealthy wanderers waiting to buy the place
will pay for. They keep going higher while
those washed up on the shore below
hope for more than a shadow to cover them.

Bright

Walk is bright this morning
in the wake of an absent
orange-eater who has scattered
sunspecks across gray stones
among nicotine yellow
cigarette butts, leaves
brown yellow red green,
scraps of slick astrobrite
brochures, a break in the clouds,
and a pink flurry of bougainvillea
petals left by early morning rain.

Far Enough

In the intermittently Euclidian space
of cities, parallel lines may intersect
if you follow them far enough.
      The only way
to know is to follow one
far enough. Riemann's map is no
better. The whole thing could go flat
in time, and you would find yourself
thinking n dimensions when you should
be thinking two, lost in lines
that appear to be points, planes
that appear to be
lines, lines that lie
side by side and do not think
forever far enough.

Cities of Conversation

for Amy

In Guangzhou, when I have to use a cellphone
to arrange a meeting with a friend, I become
one of those postmodern peripatetics snatching shards
of conversation from the air on a busy street.
I wonder how she can hear me when
I speak as though she were
walking beside me but she isn't, and there
is nothing to speak into. I hear only parts
of what she says, and I think we have become
adept at restoring cities of conversation from
broken remnants, finding our way in them
with an imprecision we learned
to tolerate by degrees when the cities were still
standing but had begun to crumble.

Cool

Clouds gathering on
a day like today are one
part hope, two parts cruel joke.
We know they carry steam
hot as the air it may soon
fill, but in the moment when
they cover the sun, we can
pretend that we are cool.

Fireworks

This is a child city that cannot stay out of the mud,
so the shower last night didn't do any good
except for the faint sweet odor it left in the air
early this morning. When it sees a puddle,
it cannot resist splashing in, and then the red
dust that is scattered everywhere becomes new
mud clinging to the city's feet that makes it
easy to track. It follows the windchime
laughter of young girls and children who wear
squeaky shoes so their parents can always hear
where they are. And the sound itself becomes
such a source of fascination that the child marches
round and round, stepping high to get the full effect until
the sound is everywhere and it mixes with laughter
of ten thousand tiny bells dancing on wind
and a marimba chorus of insects over
a few hardy birds who sing through it long after
most of their number have given up. There
is a different music coming from every door
on this street lined with bars, and if you listen
you can find the edge where they all melt

in the sun and run together with engine sounds,
sandals slipping on pavement, wind in trees, horns
or the high screech of brakes straining when
horns fail to move their target.
Fireworks for the ears,
rising to the limit of vision, visible
as absence at the corner of the eye, no face when
you turn to to face it. Your ears can
scarcely take their eyes off it.

Small Hands

nobody,not even the rain,has such small hands
e e cummings

It surprised me

when they

did not understand

the small hands

of love and rain

in this place. Perhaps

it is because the hands

of rain are so often

clenched when

they fall here.

        But this morning,

its open fingers are so

tiny you do not know

it is their touch until you

have walked a long way

with no umbrella

and see that you

are soaked through.

It Passes

At the pace of time passing, an old man
an old woman make their way
across our walk slowed already
in conversation, in time,
       by stuttering improvisation
with a partner not yet familiar. You
wait for the interval of my
step, I
          for yours,
    between us
we make
         time
for age that follows walls
like a wary cat
while we memorize
the rhythm   learn
to translate   thoughts

          The city
is an old man who smiles at youth
but knows age will outlast it, find it

creeping one day to the wall,

sitting with Buddha outside

the temple gate breathing incense,

accepting alms, blessing all

who inhabit the scene as

it passes, as

it passes.

Guangdonghua

In the shadow of Saõ Paulo's facade,
there is an unassuming temple
with a shrine to Kun Iam. I pause
for a breath of soothing incense
and nod to the goddess whose smile
is not altered by passing occupations.
A few steps away, a different incense,
thick smoke from strong cigarettes
preferred by the crowd in a small cafe
that recalls, like Saõ Paulo, a time
when Portuguese was *putonghua* here.

      To honor Li Mateou, I order
Italian pizza, drink German beer for
my ancestors. I follow the music
of two young women who speak
Portuguese at the next table. When
three pass speaking *Guangdonghua*,
I wonder why anyone would want
the whole world to sing the same song.

Endless Umbrellas

Silent supervisors of the city's
       making –
old man walks slowly,
hands clasped behind back,
stops at each site, gazes
through an opening
in the wall
surrounding it, thinks
it is not the way
it would have been
when, hesitates
between wonder and contempt
at the machinery and the young men
operating it, who look
like children playing at construction
with extravagant tinkertoys,
returns to his walk, bent
under the weight of a hard generation
and well-worn dreams of China
made new.
       Dog sits at a factory gate,

tongue hanging from a smile
that never fades, watches workers
who have moved in
from distant mountains
to refurbish the park next door.
They make miniatures to remember places
they left. He is the memory of this place,
never moves far from it, but the world
moves and moves the line of his vision.
Guards at *hai shang shie jie* run for cover
when the rain starts; women who sweep
the square there join them
while beggars gather
bowls and crutches, run
for the canopy of the bus stop,
nothing to do now but watch
and wait. But nothing
can outwait rain. This will be
a day of endless umbrellas.

Fallen Prose

Prose enough to fill an autumn
fell last night from trees shaken by wind.
Sweepers who rose with the sun
and *bai tou weng* sing brown
yellow orange red to poetry on gray stone
green grass earth the color of rust. When
the arc of fallen prose curves across a line
of sand between paving stones, it bends
light starlike. Eyes see slant.

What I Have Given

yu ren mei gui yu li xiang
If I give a person roses, their fragrance stays with me.

Know the world by a nose,

fabric woven of give

and take.

       This morning, it is

diesel at every intersection, flash

of a woman's perfume,

garbage in the sun too long, incense

burning in a temple or a loo, a factory

upwind. The cat who waits

on the walk outside my door knows

me, but she does not speak until

she smells my hand to see

what I have given.

Origami

Seeing with body,
a dancer's stillness
is origami in air,
paring an apple that is not
there, licking sticky sweet juice
from fingers when she puts down
the knife, sewing delicate cloth
with thread so fine it is nothing.
A dancer's stillness,
a string sighing to be
touched, a reed breathing to be
song.

A Promise of Divinity

Head to head above a line of ants,
two young girls share secrets that might be
in any language except the one the ants speak.
They are watching the progress of a world smaller
than they can imagine themselves being, and they
laugh at the disproportion of the burdens
below them. One blocks the path
with a foot; then, tempted by a promise
of divinity, they crush one life after
another, leaving theologically inclined
survivors to contemplate theodicies
to contain their incomprehensible whispers
and the terror of their secret smiles.

No Self

A chicken is an egg's way of making more eggs.

We are built as gene machines and cultured as meme machines,
but we have the power to turn against our own creators. We,
alone on earth, can rebel against the tyranny of the selfish
replicators.
        Richard Dawkins, The Selfish Gene

Buddha knew it takes a self to be

selfish, so he did not trust

the thing. *Consider,*

he might have said,

the gene. It toils not,

neither does it

reap. It is no

self, no desire,

no suffering, no

more than it is. Or

he might have

held a flower, silent.

                But the point

is, the point is, the point is not

the pointing: the moon. The gene is,

---

the body becoming, mind
out of body being
desire leads nowhere
but suffering. The gene, no
self, desireless, survives.

Six Note Song

A bird sings six note song
at sunrise; leaves gather
in dry clusters, whisper
when morning breeze rises.
An old woman swept there
by the same wind raises
a bowl when wealth passes
no less wanting than she.
Blind lead blind, need begs need,
absence gathers in dry
clusters, whispers a song
composed of six notes, not
whether wanting but what,
and silence on silence.

The Pace of Desire

Two monks in gray
are walking meditation
at the speed of Incheon,
an American and a Korean,
judging from appearances,
                laughing
as they pass a sign
that says *Last Chance*
to Shop and a last call
for JFK drifts over them
in Korean.
           It seems they have no reason
to fear last chances or last calls,
and they chat at the pace of desire.

When I see them later on the plane,
their bags are simple but full,
and they plunge into the clutter
with the rest of us.

Time and Again

An old woman insistent as rain
stands at my table, presses
her begging bowl between
me and the poem I have been
writing. Without a thought,
I wave her away; but she does not
move, and I look up. Meeting her eyes,
there is nothing to be done
but to place a coin in the bowl
and thank whatever gods are patient
enough to wait time and again
on my reluctant humanity.

Sudden

for Robert

Translucent rainbow wings
signal a more delicate thing
than this white-bellied beetle
who flew onto my balcony
to die. Wings lie flat against
gray, still traces of iridescence.

      At the last moment,
he turns his bright side
to the world. It lies
in a corner like a moon
reflecting sun.

      Death's surprise
prompts why, not where
or when. Slow, it is
similitude of knowing. Sudden,
too perfect for a reflecting thing to bear.

Four Parts

Sound of pilings deep as the height
of the building they are driven
to hold is doubled by an echo
off a wall to the west, joined in half
a step by east, harmony of percussion
in three parts;
      and the fourth is earth that moves
beneath the pounding of the pile driver,
slow vibration of a heavy string
your feet hear, your ear can't place.

Elegance

A scattering of clear jewels
has gathered on the right side
of a long leaf after a night
of rain, fallen from a string
broken in a downpour, gathering
the deep tropical green of a tree
not quite at home in a container
kept at a sidewalk cafe
as they would on the string
gather the soft tone
of a woman not quite at home
in the illusion of elegance.

The Tree in Guimiao Village

The Tree in Guimiao Village
prompted a conversation
about the sacredness of trees
and, in the face of cities
that cut through whatever
lies in their way, the significance
of moving them. In Cantonese
tradition, I am told, to move the tree
is to move its *feng shui* with it –
not to mention, I think, its light
and shade.

The one that came down
outside my window in Chicago left me
exposed, as though the very possibility
of shelter against sun and city's sharp edges
had been taken, its *feng shui* piled
in a landfill like fragments of a house
somebody once lived in.

I have sat *shiva* with the squirrels in mourning for it.

Mu 木

Trees like these doing handstands
among hibiscus flowers
must have been the models
for the first *mu*. Fingers
in damp clay, they wiggle green toes
two shades lighter than branches over
passersby who still wear shoes

                        in Spring. Their
root skirts hang around their ears
while they laugh and consider cartwheels.

Constellations

Tree by the footbridge is an orange galaxy
burst from primordial green
marked by constellations
of asterisks waiting for another summer;
but not today. Clouds so heavy
they sink before rain
can fall obscure low southern hills
that pass as mountains by the harbor
here. It is hard to tell
if what is on the breeze is chill
or rain so close to earth it lies
on everything, leaves no place to fall.

A Different City

Thirty minutes and it is a different
city. Everything begins at once,
but before the beginning the street
is near
      calm.
            There is room
for nothing at intervals in traffic still
building speed, but an army of workers
marches toward *She Kou Wo Er Ma*
to change that. Nothing is hard
to commodify; it breeds in silence
that gathers in low places
where morning stands; it carries
the fever that makes birds sing.

When the city rises,
it will see to this.

Steven Schroeder is a poet and philosopher who teaches and writes in Chicago and Shenzhen, China. He grew up in the Texas Panhandle, and his poetry continues to be rooted in the experience of the Plains, which teaches attention to "nothing that is not there" but more especially to "the nothing that is." His poetry has appeared or is forthcoming in the *Cresset, Georgetown Review, Halcyon, Karamu, Mid-America Poetry Review, New Texas, Poetry East, Rhino, Texas Review,* and other literary journals. His most recent collection is *Revolutionary Patience*, published by Virtual Artists Collective in 2004.

Printed in the United States
72111LV00004B/313-360

9 780977 297412